rom left: José María Hinojosa, Juan Centano, Federico García Lorca, Emilio Prados, Luis on-Daniel, at the Residencia circa 1924. Photograph from the archives of the García Lorca Foundation, courtesy of Alfonso Sánchez Rodríguez.

BLACK TULIPS

The Selected Poems
of José María Hinojosa

Translated by Mark Statman

Printed in the United States of America

José María Hinojosa

Black Tulips

Translated by Mark Statman

ISBN: 9781608010882

Library of Congress Control Number:

2012943163

UNOPRESS

University of New Orleans Press
unopress.uno.edu

Managing Editor: Bill Lavender
Book and cover design: Lauren Capone
Cover art by Katherine Koch

Acknowledgements

Some of these translations have appeared in *Tin House, Washington Square Review, Inventory, Occasional Religion* and *Ezra*. In addition, an earlier version of the introduction appeared in Tin House.

I want to acknowledge the support of my friends, colleagues and the administration at Eugene Lang College, The New School for the Liberal Arts, as well as the Provost's Office of The New School for providing student research assistance.

I have had many readers who have advised and counseled me on *Black Tulips*. I want to begin by thanking my friend and brother in poetry, Pablo Medina, with whom I translated García Lorca's *Poeta en Nueva York/Poet in New York*. This translation is dedicated to him not only for his careful reading of several versions of *Black Tulips*, but for all I have learned from him about translation and poetry through the years. It was while translating García Lorca that I first discovered the work of José María Hinojosa. This discovery led me to Alfonso Sánchez Rodríguez, editor of Hinojosa's complete works in Spanish. During our growing friendship, Alfonso provided me with insight into the world of Hinojosa for which I am grateful. Alfonso also was of valuable assistance in connecting me with the poet's heirs and I am equally grateful, as well, to them for their support of this translation.

In addition, I thank my colleagues at ALTA (American Literary Translators Association) for their interest in and suggestions for this work, in particular Alexis Levitin. Thanks as well to Jonathan Cohen and Willis Barnstone for their readings of *Black Tulips*, Willis in particular for his insightful preface. I thank my wife, Katherine, and my son, Jesse, who have probably heard one too many "new" versions of the poems here, for their love and those ears. Many thanks, too, to Bill Lavender and the University of New Orleans Press. And many thanks to Lauren Capone for her splendid design work, her incredible patience, and a primary reason for the beauty of this book. And a special tip of the cap to Peter Thompson for his superb editing of this work. I have been blessed over the years with many fine editors and it is with gratitude that I add him to this list.

A Note on the Engaged Writers Series

"Going into publishing is like entering a crisis. And it's good that this is so; crisis animates publishing."

Peter Thompson

This perspective, of the late Hubert Nyssen, motivates the Engaged Writers Series. Its mention here is not to suggest that the publishing ventures of University of New Orleans Press are undergoing the tensions felt by Nyssen when he started the French house Actes Sud. We do mean to suggest that there is a dire trend in American publishing: despite the enormous number of titles, literature is a decreasing proportion—and literature in translation hovers below 2% of the total. Moralists have called this a scandal; we activists call it a crisis.

In recent days translation has answered activism's call. Theorists such as Gayatri Spivak and Wangui wa Goro view translation as a mediation which can counterbalance (though it can also aggravate) imbalances of power. Wangui wa Goro has recently (*Journal of The African Literature Association*, Spring/Summer, 2011) spoken of translation as an activism in political "North/South" or "developed/developing" relations, as well as in purely literary contexts. The Engaged Writers Series—and UNO Press—make the wager that translation not only animates language and thought, but also rights imbalances of recognition and ignorance. It brings back the dead and martyred. It is a citric squirt against the heavy eyelid of the American reader. More than just an *aqua regia*—the only compound that can dissolve the gold of a work's "original version"—translation dissolves linguistic and cultural constructs. By placing two languages together in suspension, by weighing their failures and seeing Walter Benjamin's (*The Task of The Translator*) "pure language" through the filigree of these failures, translators dissolve constructs which steal the power of thought. The translator—perhaps more often than the original artist—sidesteps conventional formulations which are both over-determined and determining. With this in mind, UNO Press and The Engaged Writers Series produce a higher proportion of their publications in translation than all but a handful of American presses.

The Series publishes writers engaged in polemic and public struggle, along with those who engage cultural production with explicit discussion of culture. Radicals who—like their comrades André Breton, Ezra Pound, Antonin Artaud, Léopold-Sédar Senghor—insist on new definitions of culture and artistic production, or on a new connection between culture and political thesis. We are proud to include the first English translation of José Maria Hinojosa, Mark Statman's elegant collection, *Black Tulips.*

Hinojosa generally kept politics out of his poetry. Still, we are struck by his production occurring during the turbulence of the Spanish Republic. He is a suggestive companion to Antonio Gamoneda, first translated for this Series, because he was silenced at the beginning of the Civil War just as Gamoneda was silenced for decades by its outcome. There is no way to read even his most peaceful imagery without picturing the starvation, hatred and anarchy that surrounded the writer. So this book lives in the tension between opposites. His image, like much of surrealist poetry, is produced between Hegelian poles. His life was destroyed between the political poles that ravaged Spain in 1936. He was not silent about political events, and his bullet came from republicans, the polar opposite of the falangists who shot Lorca. The quiet poetry in *Black Tulips*—so long hidden from English readers—now sounds an eerie motif for an epoch that has produced hundreds of volumes of civic debate.

for Pablo Medina

Contents

Contents

La rosa de los vientos (1926)

Orillas de la luz (1927)

The Rose of the Winds (Compass) (1926)

Shores of Light (1927)

La sangre en libertad (1931)

Blood in Freedom (1931)

Foreword

Willis Barnstone

José María Hinojosa fell young with a bullet, losing both pen and memory. In this act of restoration, Mark Statman brings the Andalusian poet alive. Hinojosa's first love is the land, as was true for his compatriots Antonio Machado and Lorca. "Land, only the land," as Pedro Salinas writes. In the early poems the earth of the fields is there in the midst of diverse creeping and flying nature. The land is also the gravity of his later work. How can we forget a poet who gives us the magnificently plain and elemental lyric, "Boredom," which in severe Andalusian black and white planes, gathers body, death, and exile into relentless time. Statman's exquisite version is our gift:

Boredom

I have clothed my body
in white.

My heart
is dressed in black.

To see if I'd break through,
I sent my thought
against the haze of the old.

It fell, bounced,
broke into small pieces.
It nailed itself in me.

Unable to hold back
the leap of time,
it leaves me a rider on the land.

By his second book, Hinojosa leaves the sugarcane meadow and harsh steppe of lower Andalusia and looks elsewhere. Like his contemporary from the seaport of Cádiz, Rafael Alberti, author of *Marinero en tierra–Sailor on Dry Land*, Hinojosa finds his force in the sea—but not without discovering forests of light on the seafloor. In the end, all Spaniards, and especially Andalusians, see nothing in the world without a layer of wit. Sancho Panza, not grave don Quijote, dominates their eyes and their caustic tongue. The great poets, like Emily Dickinson, know how to handle tragedy, always imminent, with huge iron whimsy: She gives us, "Because I could not stop for Death, /He kindly stopped for me." Hinojosa's poem, "Wind in the Forest," presumes a wood somewhere on land. But no, that wood forest appears at the bottom of the sea. Then, mysteriously, the trunk of a man's body appears. We know nothing more but somehow that body, amid a storm that "wrinkles the atmosphere," instigates a diving suit to plunge. Find a drowned body? We don't know. The poem reveals only a mystery of hints. Yet without a drowned man down there in the water forests, why all those signs? After the diving suit plunge, "Green Waves" now written in caps, are somehow above the storm. What dominion is above the atmosphere in our galaxy? A good poet, Hinojosa leaves the poem as an incantatory psalm that must goes on. The best poems have no endings:

Wind in the Forest

Light at the bottom of the sea
is the light of forests.

The body of a man
is always one trunk more.

Light at the bottom of the sea
and above the storm.

Wrinkling the atmosphere
green waves come,
green waves go.

They wear a diving suit
of silence and quiet,
the bodies of crystal.

And above the storm,
Green waves come.
Green waves go.

By the time of his last volume of poems, *Blood in Freedom* (1926), the poet has gone through distinct literary adventures. In France as a student at the Sorbonne he encounters the main Spanish and French experimental poets. He already has an extensive friendship with Dalí and Buñuel. His Generation companions are all drifting into Creationism, Ultraism, and Surrealism. He plays a bit with the avant-garde moments. And he goes off to the Soviet Union. He returns unimpressed, and political writing in verse is not to be in the cards. Not yet, and the yet never happens, because of his execution. But he does enter new terrains. In *Blood in Freedom* poems there is underlying apprehension of a new period of violence. I think of no lines that say this with more rigor, and also in his uniquely allusive and elliptical style. Here is the ending of the poem, "Wings are made for flying":

Before dawn
a white dove will come to leave blood on our roof
and that blood, curdled, by noon will be our skin.

Alas, his prophecy of violence is himself. He becomes the skin of curdled blood. In this splendid book the heart of a young Andalusian from the Generation of 1927, which gives us the greatest rebirth of Spanish literature since the sixteenth-seventeenth century "Golden Age" of John of the Cross and Cervantes. I hope this volume will begin a new period for Hinojosa; that we, among the descendants from that Tower of Babel, who are still scattered over the earth with multiple tongues, including English, will know him in the crafted English poetry he merits.

Translator's Introduction

Mark Statman

For a number of years, I've been interested in the work of Spain's famed Generation of '27, in particular the poets: Federico García Lorca, Rafael Alberti, Luis Cernuda, Miguel Hernández, and Vicente Aleixandre. These are men whose lives are dramatically changed by the demise of the second Spanish Republic and the Spanish Civil War. Lorca is murdered in 1936 by the Nationalists. Hernández, dies of tuberculosis in jail, in 1942. Cernuda and Alberti go into exile. Aleixandre manages to survive Franco's attempts to destroy Spanish culture and wins the Nobel Prize for Literature in 1977, two years after Franco's death.

It was, however, with some surprise that I discovered another poet of that generation, one whose work struck me as being as powerful and evocative as his contemporaries: José María Hinojosa. In biographies of others, his name comes up in passing (he was with Buñuel and Dalí in Paris, he associated with Lorca in Madrid). Who was he? What had happened that this gifted poet was so unknown? Not only is his work un-collected and un-selected in English, but for many years his work was out of print even in Spain

That story is in his story. Hinojosa was born in 1904, in rural Campillos, to a wealthy farming and ranching family. Catholic and conservative, he was, like Lorca and Alberti, drawn to the mystery of the Spanish campo. In 1923, he went to study in Madrid where he became part of the city's growing artistic life. His family's politics and religion would prevent him from studying at the famously progressive Residencia de Estudiantes; still, as a young poet, he couldn't help being drawn to it: here one would find Lorca, Buñuel, Dalí.

Hinojosa, like many of the Generation of '27, was strongly influenced by Breton's *Surrealist Manifesto* (1924). Like Lorca and Alberti, Hinojosa's style underwent a significant change: he became less a poet of the campo and with *Poesía de perfil* (1926) and *La rosa de los vientos* (1927) we see an emerging surrealist, following Breton's ideas on the unconscious, on Hegelian idealism. In 1927, Breton issued his second manifesto in which he argued that a true surrealist must also be a communist. This argument ran counter to the beliefs of the conservative, religious Hinojosa. Still, he took Breton seriously and in 1928 visited Stalin's Soviet Union. Hinojosa returned, disturbed with the "accomplishments" of the revolution. He continued his work as a poet however, publishing three more books: *Orillas de la luz* (1928), *La flor de California* (1928), and *La sangre en libertad* (1931) where we see the poet at his most surreal.

La sangre en libertad was his last book of poetry—disenchanted with the Republic's liberalism and connections with the Soviet Union, he began, by 1932, to work against it. As an artist, he became persona non grata in particular with those very contemporaries who believed so strongly in the importance of unifying the Republic. He became deeply involved in politics—for a while he held several elected public positions. His letters from the period show little interest in literature—they are more devoted to what he sees as the critical errors of the Republic and, interestingly enough, to love and courtship. Although Hinojosa had been at the center of Spain's surrealist movement in the late 1920's and early 1930's—he was a founder with the Manuel Altologuirre of the seminal literary magazine *littoral* (still in existence today)—the political works suggests an abandonment of the surrealist principles set out by Breton. These principles, built around the dream work of Freud, the idealism of Hegel, and the social justice of Marx, no longer seemed to have any relevance to the larger issues he faced as a wealthy, landowning politician. His growing involvement with the monarchist and fascist factions of those who opposed the Republic made it difficult for him to support an artistic movement which seemed so antithetical to his class and his deeply held religious convictions. Like Dalí he worried that the general chaos of the early Republic would only be destructive to and for the Spain he deeply cherished (that Dalí was able to seemingly live on both sides of the question is, of course, another subject completely).

Eventually, his work against the Republic made him a target for anarchist forces who, in 1936, imprisoned him. On August 22, those anarchists, and other supporters of the Republic attacked the prison, assassinating Hinojosa, along with his father and brother. They also burned down his house, destroying his library and any literary work he may have done in the years between 1931 and 1936. This murder took place only three days after the murder of Lorca. There is nothing to suggest anything more than coincidence; it does, however, show how during this unstable, hopeful, and ultimately destructive period, crimes were committed by Republicans and Nationalists alike.

With that death, José María Hinojosa all but disappears from Spanish culture for half a century. For supporters of the Republic, destined for defeat, exile, and death, he becomes a kind of footnote. For supporters of Franco, he was an awkward anomaly —a sophisticated surrealist poet, even one as gifted as Hinojosa, had no proper place in the backward culture the dictator's regime would bring to post-Republic, post-war Spain. It was not until 1997 that Hinojosa's letters, thanks to the efforts of Alfonso Sánchez and Julio Neira appear in print. *Litoral* does publish a version of his selected poems in 1974 but it is not until 1998, again through the efforts of Alfonso Sánchez, that his *Obra completa* (1923-1931) appears.

It is interesting and strange for me to translate the poetry of José María Hinojosa. His right-wing conservatism stands in marked contrast with my own left, progressive biases. But he is not a political poet—it is only in some of the later poems of *La sangre en libertad* that the reader encounters his developing political vision. As a poet, he is more like his contemporaries, more like Lorca and Alberti. He is a poet who grew from writing of Spain through its folk traditions to one whose vision became newer, more complex, contemporary. He is a poet who should have left, and may still leave, a major mark on Spanish literature. To lose his work, to lose the poet, is an injustice I think must be undone. He is a poet of innovation and imagination, who played close attention to language and image, who seems a cross between the visions of surrealism and a Pound-like modernism, a poet who examines the world to find in the ordinary the mysterious.

A Note on the Translation:

Black Tulips is meant as an introduction to Hinojosa's work and represents perhaps one-third of the poems in the *Obra completa* (1923-31). I have not included any of the prose-poems from *La flor de California* which, radical at the time and certainly rich today, took me further from the poet's work than I presently wished to go. It seemed to me that the more I translated them, the more the strange and anachronistic qualities made them seem more like my contemporary imitations of Hinojosa's prose-poems than substantive translations of the works themselves. Since my hope is that *Black Tulips*, in representing an introduction to José María Hinojosa, will spark further interest in this major figure of the Generation of '27, it will be possible in the future to translate the complete poems of the poet which would allow for the inclusion of the oddly visionary *La flor de California*.

BLACK TULIPS

José María Hinojosa

Poem of the Country (1924)

Poema del Campo (1924)

Poemas para alguien

I.

Montaña nevada
sin huellas.

Mar
en calma.

Cielo
con estrellas.

II.

¿Qué será?

Águila
o aeroplano,
en lo alto
del cerro ahumado.

III.

Bosque negro
mojado
en viento.

IV.

Torvisco
fresco.

Almoraduj
oliente.

Dame tu olor
para siempre.

Poems for someone

I.

Snow covered mountains
unmarked.

Sea
in calm.

Sky
with stars.

II.

What can it be?

Eagle
or airplane
in the height
over the smoky hill.

III.

Black woods
wet
from the wind.

IV.

Flax-leafed daphne
fresh.

Sweet fragrant
marjoram.

Give me your fragrance
forever.

V.

Mimbre
frondosa.

No la dejes
sola
con el viento.

Que se vuelve
loca.

VI.

Granado.
¿Por qué no das
tu fruta
desnuda?

VII.

Una flor amarilla.
dentro de la aulaga.

Un erizo
nos impide tocarla.

Cerco
de manos rotas.

Deseo
sin timón
junto a la costa.

V.

Leafy
willow.

Don't leave it
alone
with the wind.

To go
mad.

VI.

Pomegranate tree.

Why don't you give us
your naked
fruit?

VII.

A yellow flower
inside the gorse.

A prickle
won't let us touch it.

Ring
of broken hands.

Rudderless
desire
alongside the coast.

VII.

Flor
de manzano
seca.

Manzanita
cuajada
a medias.

IX.

La higuera
dio su fruto.

La higuera
dio su sangre.

Sus ramas
se retuercen lentas
y se secan.

X.

Entre
la hierba
verde,
hojorascas podridas.

En la reguera,
sobre mastranzos,
un cínife sin vida.

XI.

La tarde se ha olvidado
por una vez tan solo
de pintarse los labios.

VIII.

Dry flower
of apple
tree

Little apple
half
ripe.

IX.

The fig tree
gave its fruit

The fig tree
gave its blood.

Its branches
twist slowly
and dry.

X.

Between
the green
grass
rotten leaves.

In the canal
above the mint
a lifeless mosquito

XI.

The afternoon has forgotten
for one time only
to paint its lips.

Por una vez tan solo
he dejado flotando
una cinta en el aire.

XII.

Suenan en mi alma
tilines de rosas,
y al campanear,
se deshojan.

XIII.

Un pino solo
en la llanura inmensa,
y en el pino,
una cigüeña.

XIV.

Panal
sin labios.

Su miel
cae en mi costado
y desgrana el pasado.

For one time only
it left floating
a ribbon in the air

XII.

Rose chimes
sound in my soul
and when they ring
their petals fall.

XIII.

A pine tree alone
in the immense plain
and in the pine
a stork.

XIV.

Honeycomb
without lips.

Its honey
falls on my side
and clears the past

Cancíon final

A Rafael Alberti

Y qué se me importa a mí
que la helada se deshiele.

Y qué se me importa a mí
que los pájaros no vuelen.

Y que los barcos más barcos,
sólo por la mar naveguen.

Si tengo en ciernes un campo
de margaritas de nieve.

Last Song

to Rafael Alberti

And what does it matter to me
if the freeze thaws.

And what does it matter to me
if the birds do not fly

And that only the ships of all ships
sail the ocean.

Because I have a field where
snow daisies bloom.

Campo

A Salvador Dalí

Olivos,
encinas,
pinos.

Campo recio,
campo de cultivo.

Encinas,
en campo bravío.

Olivos,
en campo sumiso.

Los pinos
son vigías
del campo
dormido.

Pinos,
encinas,
olivos.

Field

to Salvador Dalí

Olive trees,
evergreens
pine trees.

Hard field,
worked field.

Evergreens
in wild field.

Olive trees
in submissive field.

The pine trees
are the look-outs
for the sleeping
fields.

Pine trees,
evergreens,
olive trees.

Madrugada

Los olivos
por la mañana
dan sombra blanca.

El suelo se cubre
de una gasa
de escarcha.

Y el pegujal
se tapa
con gotas de agua.

Early Morning

The olive trees
in the morning
cast a white shadow.

A gauze
of frost
covers the land.

With drops of water
the farm
is covered.

Estelas

Almendros en flor.

La primavera
se acerca.

Cerezos en flor.

La primavera
está plena.

Granados en flor.

Ya se aleja
la primavera.

Trails

Almonds in flower.

Spring
approaches.

Cherries in flower.

Spring
complete.

Pomegranates in flower.

Already
Spring drifts away.

Encina

A Juan Vicéns

Encina,
hija
de la tierra virgen.

De brazos
desmesurados
y sublimes.

Gesto
serio
y triste.

Tronco
añoso
y firme.

El peso
de los años muertos
te redime.

Evergreen

for Juan Vicéns

Evergreen,
daughter
of the virgin earth.

Of arms
boundless
and sublime.

Movement
serious
and sad.

Trunk aged
and steady.

The weight
of dead years
redeems you.

Elegía del rocio

Una gota
de agua,
engendra un sol,
sobre las hojas
del pegujal,
después de la rociada.

Una gota de agua
qué poco es
y qué pronto se acaba.

Elegy of the Dew

A drop
of water,
breeds a sun,
over the leaves
of the farm,
after the shower.

A drop of water
so small
and quickly gone.

Sequía

a Luis Buñuel

Los árboles negros
cruzan
sus ramas,
pidiendo
un poco de agua.

Los árboles negros
clavan
su mirada
en el cielo.

A los árboles negros
no les cae agua,
y casi secos,
fijan sus ojos
en la tierra sin jugo
y sin aliento.

Drought

to Luis Buñuel

The black trees
cross
their branches
pleading
a little water.

The black trees
fix
their vision
on the sky.

No water falls
on the black trees
and almost dry
they fix their eyes
on the sapless
breathless earth.

Mies

A José Bergamín

Dedales de grano
con barbas
de franciscano.

Sábana de miel
batida
por el viento solano.

Las espigas
arrullan
el canto del verano.

Un silencio de aire
da silencio
a los campos.

Segador de cantares,
mete tu hoz
en los pegujares
y corta en sazón
el canto de los mares.

Harvest

to José Bergamín

Thimbles of grain
with
Franciscan beards.

Sheets of honey
shaken
by hot winds.

These ears of grain
court
the song of summer.

A silence of air
makes silent
the fields.

Reaper of songs
place your scythe
in these fields
and cut in their time
the song of the oceans.

Ermita

Perdida
en medio del campo,
la ermita
sólo tiene
una esquila,
para llamar
al pastor,
al gañán,
y a la beata dormida
en una choza
con techo
de paja podrida.

Hermitage

Lost
in the middle of the field
the hermitage
has only
a cattle bell
to call for
the shepherd,
the farm-hand
and the holy one asleep
in a hut
with roof
of rotten straw.

Brisa

A Rafael Busutil

La brisa
husmea
en los árboles.

Cadencia
suave.

La brisa
rasga
el aire.

Cadencia
suave.

La brisa
levanta
relámpagos de ruido
en los maizales.

Mar dormido.

Cadencia
monótono y constante.

Breeze

to Rafael Busutil

The breeze
sniffs around
in the trees.

Soft
rhythm.

The breeze
tears up
the air.

Soft
rhythm.

The breeze
raises
noisy lightning flashes
in the corn fields.

Sleeping sea.

Rhythm
monotone and constant.

Trama

A Gabriel G. Maroto

Surge
en la rama
silenciosamente
la trama.

Trama blanca.

Un legion
de arañas
sentó su campamento
en la enramada.

El olivo
aplaza
su color gris,
mientras la trama cuaja.

Flor blanca
algodonada.

Silk

to Gabriel G. Maroto

Rising
in the branch
silently
silk.

White silk.

A legion
of spiders
made camp
in the arbor.

The olive tree
delays
its gray
while the silk thickens.

White cottoned
flower.

Poetry in Silhouette (1926)

Poesía de perfil (1926)

Elegía posible

Yo solo me embarqué.
¿Adónde llegaré?

Si el globo se perdiera,
caería. ¿En qué tierra?

Si el barco naufragara,
me hundiría. ¿En qué agua?

Yo solo me embarqué.
Nadie sabe por qué.

Pero yo sí lo sé!

Possible Elegy

Alone I sailed.
Where will I arrive?

If the hot air balloon were lost,
on what land would it fall?

If the ship were to wreck,
it would sink in what waters?

Alone I started.
No one knows why.

But, I, yes I, know!

Fábula

Sustituyó a la estrella
la luciérnaga,
cuando en la tierra
hubo un rapto de luz.

Y apagó la candela
el sudor de la noche,
y la estrella fue estrella
y quedó la luciérnaga
sobre la tierra, muerta.

Fable

The firefly replaced
the star,
when on earth
there was a rapture of light.

And the sweat of the night
put out the candle,
and the star was star,
and the firefly remained
over the earth, dead.

Sueños

Embadúrnate el cuerpo
de oscuridad
y de silencio,
y podrás levantar
la copa de los sueños.

Pasaron superpuestas
ráfagas de recuerdos,
y los nuevos clisés
sólo quedan impresos,
mientras hay luz de menta
dentro del pensamiento.

Una astilla de luz
agujerea
los tulipanes negros.

Dreams

Smear your body
with darkness
and silence
and you may raise
the cup of dreams.

One over another pass
winds of memories,
only the newest clichés
leave a mark,
while inside thought
there is light of mint.

A splinter of light
pierces
the black tulips.

Entre dos aguas

a Alfonso Reyes

Buceando en la tierra
me encontré con el agua.

Con ovillo de aire
lancé la cometa,
mientras más volaba
la sentía más cerca.

Buceando en el agua,
me encontré con la arena.

La barca sin remos,
ha inflado su vela
con los horizontes
y siempre está quieta.

Between Two Waters

to Alfonso Reyes

Diving into earth
I met with water.

With a ball of air
I speared the comet
and the further it flew
the closer it felt.

Diving into water
I met with sand.

The boat with no oars
has filled its sail
with the horizons
and always is quiet.

Velocidad

Baile
de paralelas
quietas.

El paisaje
da vueltas
en la devanadera.

Ovillo
de tierra
herido
por la carretera.

Rigodón
de siluetas.

La vista avanza
como flecha
lanzada
tras la quietud suprema.

Velocity

Dance
of silent
parallels.

The landscape
strolls
in a reel.

Ball
of earth
wounded
by the road.

A dance
of silhouettes.

The view ahead advances
like an arrow
shot
toward supreme silence.

Preguntas

De puntillas,
llegaron las preguntas
por estepas de brisa.

De puntillas,
se asomaron al campo
vedado a la elegía.

De puntillas,
han tirado la piedra
que rompío la alegría.

De puntillas,
dejando su figura,
fuéronse a su guarida.

Questions

On tiptoe,
the questions came
through the grassy plain of the breeze.

On tiptoe,
they appeared in the field
forbidden to elegy.

On tiptoe,
they have thrown the stone
that shattered happiness.

On tiptoe,
leaving their figure behind,
they have left for their lair.

Sencillez

Los dedos de la nieve
repiquetearon
en el tamboril
del espacio.

Parábolas de nubes
forman un halo
de cristal
sobre el monte nevado.

Una línea
y un plano.

Quiero poner mi vista
sólo en el espacio,
que es sencillo
y a la vez complicado.

Simplicity

The fingers of snow
tap
on the small drum
of space.

Parabolas of clouds
form a halo
of crystal
above the snow covered mountain.

A line
and a plane.

I want to look
only into the space
that is simple
and at the same time complex.

Idea

Al fuego lento
templé la guitarra
de mi pensamiento.

Al fuego lento
híce una girándula
de cohetes nuevos.

Al fuego lento
oreé su espalda
a los cuatro vientos.

Lancé las semillas
a que germinaran
en llanos de cielo.

Segué con la brisa
campos florecidos
bajo el fuego lento.

Idea

By a low fire
I tuned the guitar
of my thoughts.

By a low fire
I made a spinning
of new rockets.

By a low fire
I cooled its back
to the four winds.

I threw the seeds
so they'd germinate
the fields of the sky.

Under the low fire,
I cut the flowering fields
with the breeze.

Elegía al humo de mi cigarro

Poco dura la danza.

Tejer y retejer
arabescos de seda
y mallas complicadas
para después quedar
reducido a la nada.

El aire roe tu entraña,
¡oh, blanco Prometeo!;
siempre estás amarrado
a un crepitar de fuego.

El cigarro
se destrenza el cabello
encanecido y laxo.

¡Oh, blanco Prometeo,
quién te libertará
de las garras del fuego!

Elegy for the Smoke of My Cigar

The dance doesn't last very long.

To weave and re-weave
arabesques of silk
and a complex mesh
that later
are reduced to nothing.

The air gnaws at your heart,
oh, white Prometheus!;
always fixed
to a cracking of fire.

The cigar
unwinds its hair
grown white and old.

Oh, white Prometheus,
who will free you
from these claws of fire!

Ambiente

El barco es más barco
en alta mar,
entre las olas
y el huracán

Y el águila, en el aire,
sabe mejor mirar,
embistiendo a las nubes
que le impiden volar.

Rompe los zancos
y comienza a andar
sobre la tierra,
sobre la tierra de verdad.

Atmosphere

Boat, ever more boat,
on the high sea,
between the waves
and the hurricane.

And the eagle, in the air,
can better see,
charging through the clouds
that would keep it from flying.

Break the high masts
and begin to walk
on the land,
the land of truth.

Dolor

Cuerda de guitarra
que se rompe
al templarla.

La punta de la flecha
fue untada
de tristeza.

Gira la estrella
en el vacío,
y deja deslumbrada
la caverna.

Silencio de silencio.

Ni abriendo nuevos cauces
al momento,
quita sus letanías
del desierto desierto.

El sentimiento
se vuelve más espeso.

Sorrow

The string of the guitar
breaks
when tuned.

The head of the arrow
was smeared
with sadness.

The star turns
in the void,
and leaves the cave
dazed.

Silence of silence.

Not even opening new riverbeds
in the moment
takes away the litanies
of the deserted desert.

Sentiment
grows even thicker.

Calma

A Luis Buñuel

¿Dónde se acaba el mar?
¿Dónde comienza el cielo?
Los barcos van flotando.
o remontan el vuelo?

Se perdió el horizonte,
en el juego mimético
del cielo y de las aguas.

Se fundió el movimiento,
en un solo color
azul, el azul quieto.

Se funden los colores;
se apaga el movimiento.

Un solo color queda;
no existe barlovento.

¿Dónde se acaba el mar?
¿Dónde comienza el cielo?

Calm

for Luis Buñuel

Where does ocean end?
Where does sky begin?
The boats go floating
or do they overcome flight?

The horizon was lost
in this mimetic game
of sky and waters.

The movement becomes
a single color
blue, a quiet blue.

The colors melt together;
movement ends.

A single color remains
nothing exists windward.

Where does ocean end?
Where does sky begin?

Hastío

He vestido de blanco
mi cuerpo

Mi corazón
se ha vestido de negro.

Por ver si la rompía
lancé mi pensamiento
contra la nebulosa
de lo viejo.

Y cayó rebotado,
y hecho trozos sueltos
vino a clavarse en mí.

La corveta del tiempo
no pude refrenarla,
y me dejó jinete sobre el suelo.

Boredom

I have clothed my body
in white.

My heart
is dressed in black.

To see if I'd break through,
I sent my thought
against the haze
of the old.

It fell, bounced,
broke into small pieces
it came to nail itself in me.

Unable to hold back
the leap of time,
it left me a rider on the land.

Entre dos luces

a Hernando Víñes

El azul Polifemo
fue herido por la hora
que lo ha dejado ciego;
la sangre silenciosa
manaba de su cuerpo.

Desde el poniente tiran
de una cortina negra,
con un hilo ceniza.

En un redil de niebla
han quedado cercadas
las miradas añejas.

Y la luz fué amarrada
con las cuerdas de fuego
al cuerpo de la llama.

At Twilight

to Hernando Viños

The blue Polyphemos
was injured by the hour
that left him blind;
silent blood
poured forth from his body.

From the west
a black curtain pulls
with an ashen thread.

In a foggy sheep fold
remain enclosed
aged visions.

And the light was bound
with ropes of fire
to the body of the flame.

Quietud

Albahaca
tronchada.

Sobre la rama
calla la cigarra.

Un átomo de ruido
ha caido en el agua
y ha engendrado una onda
perfecta y elástica.

Luz
en tamiz de plata.

Quiet

Sweet basil
cut.

Above the branch
the cicada is silent.

An atom of noise
has fallen on the water,
created a wave
perfect, elastic.

Light
in sift of silver.

Tristeza

A Apeles Fenosa

El bordón
sonó a hueco.

La caña transportó
un ramo de sonidos
de luna al pensamiento.

Otra vez el bordón
volvió a sonar a hueco.

El crystal se rompió
y recogí en un lirio
sus amarillos restos.

Pero el bordón,
en su último recuerdo,
se contuvo y saltó.

Sadness

To Apeles Fenosa

The pilgrim's staff
sounded hollow.

The cane transported
a branch of moon sounds
to thought.

Once more the pilgrim's staff
returned a hollow sound.

Crystal broke
and I collected in an iris
its yellow remains.

But the pilgrim's staff,
in its final memory,
stopped and leapt.

Misterio

A Francisco G. Cossío

Lame con furia el viento
la copa de los árboles,
y mientras huye lento,
les quita de su tronco
la savia del silencio.

Un espectro de barca
pasó por el reflejo,
y sacó luz del mar
al golpe de los remos.

La noche va descalza
y come con su aliento
urdimbre de ruido.

Se oyen en el puerto
bramidos de maromas
y lamentos de negros.

¿Adónde va la estrella
que patina en el cielo
y parte en dos mitades
sangrando luz su cuerpo
el manantial del aire?

Mystery

To Francisco G. Cossío

The wind licks with anger
the tops of the trees
and while it slowly flees,
takes from their trunk
the sap of silence.

A ghost of a boat
passed through its reflection
and the rhythm of its oars
took the ocean's light.

The night goes barefoot
and eats with its breath
a warp of noise.

They hear in the port
the roar of the ropes
and laments of blacks.

Where does the star go
that skates in the sky
its body, bleeding light,
splitting in two
the fountain of air?

Viento en el bosque

A Joaquín Peinado

Luz de fondo de mar
es la luz de los bosques.

Siempre es un tronco más
el cuerpo de algún hombre.

Luz de fondo de mar
y arriba el temporal.

Arrugando la atmósfera,
olas de verde vienen,
olas de verde van.

Llevan una escafandra
de silencio y quietud,
los cuerpos de cristal.

Y arriba el temporal.
Olas de verde vienen.
Olas de verde van.

Wind in the Forest

To Joaquín Peinado

The light at the bottom of the ocean
is the light of the forests.

The body of a man
is always one more trunk.

Light at the bottom of the ocean
and above the storm.

Wrinkling the atmosphere
green waves come,
green waves go.

They wear a diving suit
of silence and quiet,
bodies of crystal.

And above the storm.
Green waves come.
Green waves go.

Signos del mar

a Dario de Regoyos

El mar cierra sus brazos
y engarza al marinero,
en hilos de gris plata
y azulados fosfenos.

Sacude el mar sus plumas
en espasmos de sueño,
y arroja el horizonte
sobre el confín del cielo.

El mar abre sus brazos
y deja al marinero, entre velas y hélices,
un único recuerdo.

La costa deletrea
los mensajes del mar
los mensajes del viento,
y el amor marinero.

Signs of the Ocean

to Dario de Regoyos

The ocean closes its arms
and so binds the sailor
in gray silver threads
that flash blue inside the eyes.

The ocean shakes its feathers
in spasms of sleep
and arranges the horizon
over the confines of sky.

The ocean opens its arms
and leaves the sailor, between sails and propellers
his only memory.

The coast spells out
messages of ocean
messages of wind,
the sailor's love.

The Rose of the Winds (Compass) (1926)

La rosa de los vientos (1926)

Prólogo

29º 27'6" lat. N 5º 48'3" long. E

De todos los horizontes
brotaron poemas nuevos,
que vinieron a juntarse
en la Rosa de los Vientos,
y cada poema trajo
el recuerdo de su cielo.

Prologue

29° 27" 6" lat. N 5° 48' 3" long. E

From every horizon
appeared new poems
that came to join
the Rose of the Winds
and each poem carried
the memory of its sky

N

Para picotear sobre mi fría palma,
bajan aleteando las estrellas
y la Osa Mayor no será nunca blanca,
porque ha olvidado su pasión mimética.

Han puesto colgaduras encaladas,
para borrar los huecos de mis huellas,
mujeres negras que habitan mi casa.
Sólo han brotado de mi barco velas.

Mientras oteo curvos horizontes
en el balcón de escarcha tempranera,
veo llegar al humo desde Londres,
que amarillo nació en las chimeneas
y, cano ya, me llama a grandes voces
y pregunta con gesto anacoreta
por la senda que lleva al Polo Norte.

Encogiendo mis hombros hechos niebla,
yo le regalo un alfabeto Morse.

N

To peck on my cold palm,
the fluttering stars come down
and the Great Bear will never be white,
because it has forgotten its mimetic passion.

The blackened women who live in my house
have placed white-washed drapes
to erase the holes of my footprints.
Only sails have blossomed from my boat.

Meanwhile, on a balcony of early frost,
I look over the curved horizon,
I see the smoke of London arrive,
born yellow in the chimneys
and, now white with age, it calls me in loud voices
and asks with a hermit's gesture
for the path to the North Pole.

Shrugging my shoulders turned to mist,
I give it the gift of Morse Code.

NNE

Me desperté pensando
en las afueras de la noche
y amenecí sin tacto.

Con su risa de estrellas,
la noche ríe, ríe, ríe, ríe, ríe y ríe
con una risa histérica.

Pasaron días sin luz
y noches iluminadas,
dejando un sedimento en las cabezas
de llama casi apagada.

Y puse una bandera
de color de alegría
en medio de la linde
donde comienza el baile de mi vista,
sin temor de encontrar esos bichos que fuman
y en donde sólo viven mi aliento y mi sonrisa.

Un ritmo corpulento
descendió de la cumbre, patinando
por entre ventisqueros
y se asomó espantado por la luz
al mar Medterráneo.

NNE

I woke up thinking
in the outskirts of night
and I rose untouched.

With the laughter of the stars,
the night laughs, laughs, and laughs
the laughter hysterical laughter.

Days passed without light
illuminated nights
leaving sediment in heads
of almost extinguished flame.

And I put a flag
the color of happiness
in the middle of the border
where my eyesight's dance began
without fear of meeting those creatures who smoke
and where only my breath and smile live.

A corpulent rhythm
descended from the peak, sliding
between glaciers,
and appeared frightened by the light
of the Mediterranean Sea.

ENE

Un vals me trajo la luz de otros tiempos;
aventuras de príncipes barítonos
con cinturas delgadas, que el eco
las prendió a los cinco dedos
de mi mano derecha,
pensando en madrugadas
cubiertas por la pátina del alba.

Toqué la mandolina
con sonrisa de incrédulo
y al pasar por la noche reflejada,
amaestré las aguas a bien oír conciertos.

El manantial de Venus
brotó en dos surtidores
y regó todo el campo con su cuerpo.

Florencia pide auxilio
porque la rapta el Arno
que lleva en su corriente
hojas secas de otoños ya pasados.

Atravesé en mi huida
todo el renacimiento
y el mar me abrió sus brazos
y templó mis deseos.

ENE

A waltz brought me the light of other times;
of thin-waisted baritone princes,
and the echo of their adventures
caught by the five fingers
of my right hand,
thinking of mornings
covered in a patina of dawn.

I played the mandolin
with an incredulous smile
and throughout the reflected night
I taught the waters how best to hear these concerts.

Venus' spring
rushed two ways
and watered the fields with her body.

Florence asks help
because the Arno abducts her
carrying in its current
dry leaves of autumns past.

In my flight
I crossed the Renaissance
and the ocean opened its arms to me
and cooled my desires.

E

Teñí mi retina
de amarillo limón
y entorné los párpados
para mirar el sol.

Se ha prendido a mi vuelo
el canto de un geisha
con voz de junco
y ritmo de palmera.

"Escribió Li-tai-po
su última poesía
con burbujas de agua

en la barca sin quilla
y sobre el pergamino
combado de la orilla."

La geisha sigue su canto
ya en nenúfar transformado.

"Beberás luz de luz
antes de que la escarcha
sobre tu almendro en flor
haya puesto su planta."

Desde mi barco de bambú
vi hacer malabarismos
a los patos silvestres
con un almud de caracteres chinos.

E

I dyed my retina
a lemon yellow
and half-closed my eyelids
to look at the sun.

The song of a geisha
attached to my flight
her voice like rushes
and rhythm of palm tree.

"Li-tai-po wrote
his final poetry
with bubbles of water

in a boat with no keel
and on folded parchment
of shore."

The geisha continues her song,
her voice transformed to a water-lily:

"You will drink light of light
before the frost
has covered your flowering
almond tree."

From my bamboo boat
I saw wild ducks
juggling small sacks
of Chinese letters.

ESE

Del mar al Himalaya,
del Himalaya al mar.

Si echaran los cimientos
de una nueva Ispahán
y Omar Khayán volviera
a ser Omar Khayán,
pondría rosas negras
prendidas en mi ojal.

Dejadme vivir tranquilo,
en el aire.

Dadme un buen vaso de vino,
en el mar.

El Ganges coge en sus brazos
serpientes de la oración.
¡Quién pudiera nadar en el sol!

El Ganges abre sus brazos
para dormir sobre el mar.
¡Quién pudiera en el mar sestear!

El viento pierde su vida
oliendo flores de tierra,
en su lento caminar,
ya del mar al Himalaya,
ya del Himalaya al mar.

ESE

From the sea to the Himalayas
from the Himalayas to the sea.

If they laid the foundation
for a new Ispahan
and Omar Khayam would once again
be Omar Khyam,
there'd be pinned black roses
to my coat's lapel.

Let me live quietly,
in the air.

Give me a good glass of wine,
in the sea.

The Ganges holds in its arms
serpents of prayer.
Who could swim in the sun?

The Ganges opens its arms
to sleep on the sea.
Who could sleep over the sea!

The wind loses its life
smelling flowers of earth,
in its slow walking,
now from the sea to the Himalayas
now from the Himalayas to the sea.

SO

Subido encima de un cacto,
tararea el Amazonas
el canto del papagayo,
y porque no suene a hueco,
en silencio se ha quitado
el plumaje de su cuerpo.

El Amazonas es bromista
y apaga las flores de fuego
que florecen en sus orillas.

Los Andes mojan su cola
áspera en el agua fría
y enseñan dientes de roca.

Un indio me ha preguntado
con su voz de lengua rota
por qué voy sin taparrabo.

SW

Bright above a cactus
the Amazon hums
the parrot's song,
and because so soft one can't hear
in silence it has lost
the feathers of its body.

The Amazon is a trickster
and blows out the flowers of fire
that bloom on its banks.

The Andes wet their rough tail
in the cold water
and reveal their rocky teeth.

Why I go without loin cloth,
an Indian asked me,
in his voice of broken tongue.

SSE

He perdido
la memoria de los siglos:
sólo conservo alientos
de papiros añejos.

Y tengo la nostalgia de mí mismo,
de cuando sabios eran mis consejos,
del tiempo en que mi olor
no era del museo.

No puedo resistir
ver correr de mis ojos
arenales de lágrimas
formados por escombros.

Yo perdí la noción del calendario
y de días microbios,
pero continuaré mi papel de hierático,
con sonrisa de insomnio,
en este film inacabado.

Mi voz, mi signo indescifrado,
no lo busquéis en el presente,
buscadlo en el pasado.

SSE

I have lost
the memory of centuries,
I only have breaths
of old papyrus.

And I have a nostalgia for myself,
for when my counsels were wise,
a time when my smell
was not of the museum.

I can't resist
to see run from my eyes
strands of tears
refuse-formed.

I lost the sense of the calendars
and of germ-filled days
but I will continue my grand role,
with a smile of insomnia
in this unfinished film.

My voice, my undeciphered sign,
don't you look for it in the present,
look for it in the past.

NNW

El mar no es el mar.
El mar está hecho
de nieve y de viento.

El mar no es el mar.
Es un archipiélago
de agua o de hielo.

Pasaron rebaños
de icebergs cubiertos
de pájaros blancos.

El mar no es el mar.
El mar es el cielo,
icefield alado,
de azul recubierto.

NNW

The sea isn't the sea.
The sea is made
of snow and wind.

The sea isn't the sea.
It's an archipelago
of water or ice.

Herds of icebergs
passed, covered by
white birds.

The sea is not the sea.
The sea is the sky,
winged ice-field
covered in blue.

Shores of Light (1927)

Orillas de la luz (1927)

Encuentro fortuito

Salieron a mi encuentro,
en una encrucijada,
su voz y sus dos ojos
cubiertos de una túnica de sombra.

Su voz, hecha pavesas por el fuego,
oprimió mi garganta
y grabó sobre el cuerpo de la noche
una huella de sangre luminosa.

Aquella noche estaba yo despierto
y vi caer sus ojos de la rama
de un árbol florecido;
y vi caer sus ojos todos abiertos
en un lago sin fondo
donde flotaba, envuelta entre reflejos,
su voz junto de mi carne,
que perdiera una noche al acostarme.

Meeting by Chance

They came out to meet me
at a crossroads
her voice and two eyes
covered by a robe of shadow.

Her voice, sparked by fire,
tightened my throat,
and engraved through the body of the night
a footprint of luminous blood.

That night I was awake
and saw her eyes fall from the branch
of a flowering tree
I saw her open eyes fall
in a bottomless lake
where, together, wrapped in reflections,
her voice floated with my flesh;
the flesh of my body,
another night I'd lost of sleep.

Unidos por la luz

Bajo una misma luz
están nuestras cabezas.

Tu corazón y el mío
cantan sobre las piedras
cuando la noche oculta
los rugidos de fieras.

¿Tu corazón y el mío eran sólo de arena?

Por el desierto arrastran los camellos sus penas
y llevan en sus ojos oasis de palmeras.

¿Tu corazón y el mío
eran sólo de arena?

Por el desierto arrastran los camellos sus penas
y llevan en sus ojos oasis de palmeras.
¿Tu corazón y el mío
eran sólo de arena?

Nuestras sombras unidas
florecen en la tierra.

United by Light

Under the same light
our heads.

Your heart and mine
sing over the stones
when the night hides
the roars of beasts.

Your heart and mine were only sand?

Through the desert, the camels pull their grief
and they carry in their eyes an oasis of palms.

Your heart and mine
only sand?

Through the desert, the camels pull their grief
and they carry in their eyes an oasis of palms.
Your heart and mine
only sand?

Our shadows united
flower on earth.

Alivio

Llevo dos luces a un tiempo,
fragmentarias,
puestas sobre mis pupilas
y corro sin detenerme
buscando por los orillas,
vanamente,
la luz que colme mi vista.

Mis huellas sobre la arena
las roba el mar con sus olas,
y mis plantas

inútilmente sembraron
sus pisadas
en un campo
tendido bajo la nieve.

Y las dos luces a un tiempo
me desgarran las pupilas
y van mis pasos al viento
y yo no encuentro a mi vista
luz para bañar mi cuerpo.

Relief

I carry two lights at a time,
fragments,
placed over my pupils
and I run without stopping
seeking on the shores
in vain,
the light that will fill my vision.

My footprints from the sand
the sea steals with its waves
and my soles

uselessly sowed
their footsteps
in a field
spread under snow.

And the two lights at a time
tear at my pupils
and my steps go with the wind
and I don't find in my sight
light to bathe my body.

Así es

Porque siempre esté la puerta abierta
y sólo esperen ver siluetas.

Porque la luz camine desnuda
y la vistan de sombras mudas.

Porque lleva el mar en su frente
y la resaca no la hiere.

Porque si en tierra hunde su cabeza
sacan luego una calavera.

Se permiten dudar
de la isla y del oasis.

The Way It Is

So that the door is always open
and they only expect to see silhouettes.

That the light walks naked
and they clothe it in mute shadows.

Because it carries the sea in its forehead
and the undertow doesn't wound it.

If your head is buried in the earth
then they will drag out a skull.

They allow themselves to doubt
island and oasis.

Atavismo

Alas de golondrinas
brotan de los castaños
y su vuelo se clava
en el juego arbitrario
de la luz y las risas
de nuestros invitados.

Aún conservo la sombra
que puesta entre mis labios
me dio un sabor de sangre
manada del costado
de diez generaciones
muertas en el Calvario.

En constante equilibrio,
cuerpos amurallados
tejieron rigodones
sin hora de descanso
conteniendo su aliento
por no empañar los campos.

Los nuevos corazones
amanecen blindados
y aquel collar de bailes
quedó roto en el acto
en que posé mis dedos
en las ramas del arbol.

Reversion

Swallows' wings
bud from the chestnut trees
and their flight is fixed
in the arbitrary game
of light and the laughter
of our guests.

Still I keep the shadow
set between my lips,
the taste of blood
from the sides
of ten generations
dead at Calvary.

In constant equilibrium
bodies surrounded
wove provincial dances
without an hour's rest,
holding their breath
to not mist the fields.

The new hearts
in armor rise
and that necklace of dances
remained broken from the moment
in which I set my fingers
in the limbs of the tree.

Hacia allí

En una espiral sube este aleteo que florece en luces de bengala y hace de mi cuerpo una bujía poblada de aves del Paraíso. Mi alma tiene sangre luminosa y voy dejando por allí donde paso un reguero de fuegos fatuos desprendidos de las astillas de mis huesos, que saltan al choque con las esquinas de las calles. Todas las calles desmbocan en el monte Calvario, y esta mujer, que lleva su dedo índice sobre los labios para apagar los fuegos fatuos, también desemboca en el monte Calvario.

Mi cuerpo sin brazos ni piernas da saltos sobre la arena de pez recién salido del mar. Este rumor de olas¿por qué llena de sangre mis ojos y de espuma mi boca?

La cita fue en el monte Calvario y una vez allí tomaremos un cock-tail reunidos ypronunciaremos nuestra última palabra.

To There

In a spiral the fluttering rose, blooming blue flowers of Bengal flares, and makes my body a candle covered by birds of paradise. My soul has luminous blood and I leave to go where the trail of will o' the wisp loosened splinters from my bones, fire that jumps with a crash at street corners. All of the streets flow to Calvary and this woman, who places her finger over her lips to put out the will o' the wisp, also flows to Calvary.

My body without arms or legs jumps over the sand of the fish that had just left the sea. This murmur of waves, why does it fill my eyes with blood and my mouth with foam?

The rendezvous was at Calvary and once there we will drink a cocktail together and deliver our final word.

Viaje con regreso

Escondido en la luz,
mi cuerpo todo luz, difumínose,
dejando un surco leve
abierto por la estela de la noche.

Nadie oye el ruido
de los pasos perdidos en tinieblas;
de mis pasos opacos
desmoronados sobre mi cabeza.

Ya preso entre paréntesis,
la luna acalla el ritmo de sus olas,
se desborda mi cuerpo
y mana espuma por sus cuencas rotas.

Cruzan de esquina a esquina
doce bustos de mármol patinado
de doce emperadores
que husmean en mi pecho esmerilado.

Busca a tientas mi mano
sus ojos y su mano de ceniza,
enlazada con yedra,
que flota sobre un agua sin aristas.

Mi cuerpo todo luz
cayó tendido en tierra calcinada
y brotaron de él
un manantial de luz y otro de escarcha.

Voyage with return

Hidden in the light
my body all light, dimmed,
leaving a slight furrow
open through the trail of night.

No one hears the noise
of the lost steps in the shadows;
of my dark steps
crumbled on my head.

Still a prisoner between parenthesis,
the moon quiets the rhythm of its waves,
it flows over my body
and foam pours from its flooded shores.

They cross from corner to corner
twelve busts of glazed marble
of twelve emperors
to peer at my polished breast.

My hand feels for
its eyes and its hand of ash,
linked with ivy
that floats above the unrippled water.

My body all light
fell to the black earth
and from it rushed
a spring of light and another of frost.

¿Por qué no?

Bañabase en la playa
sin corazón
y sin el velo de la desposada.

Y tenía su cuerpo,
sin corazón,
por la arena salada recubierto.

Tendida sobre el aire,
sin corazón,
comenzó a despojarse de su carne.

¿Y el corazón?
Los peces lo llevaban,
mar adentro, colgado en sus alas.

Why not?

She was bathing at the beach
without a heart
and without the newly-weds veil.

And her body,
without a heart
was covered by the salty sand.

Stretched out over the air
without a heart
she began to shed her flesh.

And the heart?
The fish carried it,
out to sea, suspended from their wings.

Erótica imprevista

Hundido entre juncales,
eludí la pasión
de la mujer sin carne.

Eludí la pasión,
dentro de mi ramaje
y sin quererlo yo.

Perdida entre arenales
la mujer, ya voló
mi carne con su carne.

Unexpected Erotica

Sunken between reed-beds
I escaped the passion
of the woman without flesh.

I escaped the passion
within my leaves
I without wanting to.

Lost in the great sands
the woman, still my flesh flew
with her flesh.

Tres amigos

La luz estaba a un lado
y en el otro la sombra,
uniéndolas en un arco.

Ante mi cuerpo erguido,
cogidos de la mano,
pasaron tres amigos.

Sus voces van delante
sin encontrar oídos
en donde refugiarse.

¿Dónde acaba el incendio?
Cristo lavó su carne.
¡Son brillantes mis huesos!

Three Friends

Light was on one side
and on the other shadow,
uniting them an arc.

Before my unbowed body,
united by hand,
passed three friends.

Their voices go ahead
without meeting ears
where they would be heard.

Where does the fire end?
Christ washed his flesh.
Brilliant are my bones!

Su voz Lillian Gish

Todas mis entrañas están llenas de corazones cogidos con dos dedos, con sus dos dedos doloridos de tanto crujir sus articulaciones. Con esta invasion de corazones diminutos se verá obligada Lillian Gish a abadonar su último refugio de la tierra para convertirse en este gran corazón azul que llevo suspendido sobre mi cabeza.

Lillian Gish, Lillian Gish! ¿Por qué me llena su voz de Lillian Gish?

Todos los corazones estallaban en el aire como pompas de jabon dejando en el espacio una vibración Lillian Gish que envuelve mis oídos con su voz desenfocada.

Oh, Lillian Gish, Lillian Gish! ¿Por qué me llena su voz de Lillian Gish?

Her Voice Lillian Gish

My insides are full of hearts taken with two fingers, with her two aching, creaking joints. With this invasion of small hearts, Lillian Gish will be obliged to abandon her final refuge on earth and become this great blue heart I carry suspended above my head.

Lillian Gish, Lillian Gish! The voice of Lillian Gish, why does it fill me?

All the hearts exploded in the air like soap bubbles, leaving in their place a Lillian Gish vibration that covers my ears with her unfocussed voice.

Oh, Lillian Gish, Lillian Gish! Why does it fill me, the voice of Lillian Gish?

Sin saber por qué

Por una valle de alas
llenando el Universo
viene hacia mí su cuerpo
hecho luces del alba.

De su frente caían
las estrellas audaces
y su voz tinta en sangre
paraliza mi vida.

Van mis pies temblorosos
por murallas de piedra
y en un bosque de higueras
me sorprendió el otoño.

Without Knowing Why

Through a valley of wings
filling the Universe
your body of dawn's light
comes to me.

From your forehead fell
bold stars
and your blood-tinged voice
paralyzes my life.

My trembling feet walk
by walls of stone
and in a forest of fig trees
the autumn surprised me.

Doble encuentro

Entre estos cuatro puntos se esconde todo el secreto de la arena y de las olas, de mi alma y de mi cuerpo.

Solamente las gaviotas y los niños de primera comunión pueden llevar en sus picos algo que se asemeje a la piel de la luna llena. Por eso el azul no les hiere, ni su sangre es roja. ¿Por qué degollarán tanto niño de primera comunión a orillas del mar?

Como seguían estos cuatro puntos cardinales calvados en mi frente temblaba en mis ojos un encuentro de agua y de arena, de alma y de carne.

Double Meeting

Between these four points, hides the whole secret of sand and waves, of my soul and body.

Only the seagulls and the children of first communion can carry in their beaks something similar to the skin of the full moon. That's why the blue doesn't wound them, nor is their blood red. Why will they behead every child of the first communion at the seashore?

As these four essential points remained nailed to my forehead a meeting trembled in my eyes of water and sand, of soul and flesh.

Prisión sin límites

Vuela mi corazón
unido con los pájaros
y deja entre los árboles
un invisible rastro
de alegría y de sangre.

Las gotas de rocío
se helaron en las manos
abiertas y floridas
de los enamorados
perdidos en la brisa.

Vuela mi corazón,
mi corazón atado
con cadenas de estrellas
a la sombra de un árbol
atado con cadenas
y con cantos de pájaros.

Prison Without Limits

My heart flies
along with the birds
and leaves among the trees
an invisible trace
of happiness and blood.

The dew drops
froze in the
opened and flowered
hands of the lovers
lost in the breeze.

My heart flies,
my heart bound
by chains of stars
to the shadow of a tree
bound by chains
and bird song.

Anatomía de un momento

Pasa por me memoria
suspendida en el aire
sólo un rumor de hojas
perdido entre los árboles.

Mira esta lupa negra
que divide los cuerpos
y me enseña las venas
de tu costado izquierdo.

Una lluvia muy fina
humedeció el aliento
y empañó las venillas
llenas de sal y fuego.

Pasan por mi memoria
las ramas de los árboles
con un rumor de hojas
y de ríos de sangre.

Anatomy of a Moment

Through my memory passes
suspended in the air
only the murmur of the leaves
lost between the trees.

This black magnifying glass
that divides the bodies
shows me the veins
of your left side.

A very light rain
dampened the breath
and misted the small veins
full of salt and fire.

Through my memory pass
the branches of trees
with a murmur of leaves
and rivers of blood.

Siempre ella

Precisamente porque estaba sola
tendida en una rama de la noche
no quise vadear el arco iris
para unir en un beso nuestras voces.

Ella guardaba dentro de sus ojos
una pareja de palomas blancas,
ella tenía dentro de sus párpados
la nieve derretida de sus lágrimas.

Esta noche de seda, cómo cruje
y se hace toda ecos, a mi paso,
ocultando en sus pliegues las palabras
que escapan sin querer de nuestros labios.

Precisamente porque estaba sola
yo me había disuelto con el aire,
dejó volar aquel par de palomas.

Always Her

Precisely because she was alone
stretched out on a limb in the night
I didn't want to wade the rainbow
to join our voices in a kiss.

She kept within her eyes
a pair of white doves,
she had inside her eyelids
the melted snow of her tears.

This night of silk, how it rustles
and makes everything echo, at my steps,
hidden in its folds the words
that acccidentally escape our lips.

Precisely because she was alone
I was dissolved by the air,
that pair of doves stopped flying.

Herido siempre

Herido siempre, desangrado a veces
y ocultando mi sangre sin riberas
llevo mis pasos presos entre nieblas
y mis miradas van sobre cipreses.

Aún conservo en las uñas esta sangre
que me dejó la carne de un momento
empapado de lágrimas y miedo
cuando vino a perderse entre mi carne.

Era sólo mi sangre quien llamaba
en medio de aquel valle, de aquel bosque,
y era sólo mi sangre, eran mis voces
las que oían la lluvia sobre el agua.

Always Wounded

Always wounded, bloodied sometimes
and hiding my blood without shores
I walk a prisoner between clouds
and my visions go beyond the cypress trees.

Still I preserve in my nails this blood
that left the flesh of a moment
soaked with tears and fear
when it came to lose itself in my flesh.

It was my blood only who called
in the middle of that valley, that forest,
and it was my blood only, my voices
that heard the rain above the water.

Es o no así

Con su túnica negra
avanza entre la bruma
y un relámpago rojo
corta en dos su figura.

Lleva sus cinco dedos
envueltos en luz pura
y de su boca abierta
manaba amor y dudas.

¿Es verdad que en el campo
duermen los guardagujas
atravesado el pecho
de rieles de luna?

¿Es verdad que en el campo
son verdes las preguntas?

Dentro de su pupila
saltan voces oscuras
cubiertas con la piel
de mujeres desnudas.

Con su túnica negra
avanza entre la luna;
tempestad de cabellos
metida en una urna.

¿Es verdad que en el campo
son verdes las preguntas?

It is or is not like this

In her black dress
she advances through the mist
and a red flash of lightning
cuts her figure in two.

Her five fingers are
enveloped in pure light
and from her mouth
poured forth love and doubts.

Is it true that in the country
the switchmen sleep
with the rails of the moon
across their chests?

Is it true that in the country
questions are green?

Inside her pupil
dark voices jump
covered by the skin
of naked women.

In her black dress
she advances through the moon;
storm of hair
placed in an urn.

Is it true that in the country
questions are green?

Así fue

Se cubrían mis sienes
de frutas y de pájaros
pero este olor a luz
no es siempre el mismo,
ni llevan las heladas
siempre hielo en su alma.

Ayer, mañana u hoy
seré vigía sin ojos,
que el frío y el calor
de cuanto me rodea

da secretos al tacto
de naipes enjaulados.

Se cubrieron mis sienes
de frutas y de pájaros,
cuando el hielo fue sangre
y fue la luz, bengala;
cuando el cielo y el mar
confunden sus amarras.

It was like this

My temples were covered
with fruits and birds
but this scent of light
isn't always the same
nor does the frost always carry
frost in your soul.

Yesterday, tomorrow, or today
I will be the watchman without eyes
though cold and heat
surround me

give secrets at the touch
of caged playing cards.

My temples were covered
with fruits and birds;
when the ice was blood
and the night a blue flaring Bengal light;
when the sky and sea
confused their mooring cables.

Blood in Freedom (1931)

La sangre en libertad (1931)

Ya no me besas

Un viento inesperado hizo vibrar las puertas
y nuestros labios eran de cristal en la noche
empapados en sangre dejada por los besos
de las bocas perdidas en medio de los bosques.

El fuego calcinaba nuestros labios de piedra
y su ceniza roja cegaba nuestros ojos
llenos de indiferencia entre cuatro murallas
amasadas con cráneos y arena de los trópicos.

Aquella fue la última vez que nos encontramos
llevabas la cabeza de pájaros florida
y de flores de almendro las sienes recubiertas
entre lenguas de fuego y voces doloridas.

El rumbo de los barcos era desconocido
y el de las caravanas que van por el desierto
dejando sólo un rastro sobre el agua y la arena
de mástiles heridos y de huesos sangrientos.

Aquella fue la última noche que nuestros labios
de cristal y de sangre unieron nuestro aliento
mientras la libertad desplegaba sus alas
de nuestra nuca herida por el último beso.

Now You Won't Kiss Me

An unexpected wind made the doors shake
and our lips were crystal in the night
soaked in blood left by the kisses
of mouths lost in the midst of the forests.

The fire burned our lips of stone
and its red ash blinded our eyes
full of indifference to the four dough-like walls
with skulls and sand of the tropics.

That was the last time we met,
your head filled with flowered birds
your temples covered with almond flowers
amid tongues of fire and pained voices.

The course of the ships was unknown
and that of the caravans that go through the desert
leaving only a trace over water and sand
broken masts and bloodied bones.

That was the last night that our lips
of crystal and blood united our breath
while liberty spread its wings
from our necks wounded by the last kiss.

Cuando nos miramos

Mi cabeza inclinada sobre el aire
miraba su cabeza hecha amor por mis ojos
cuando de sus cabellos
saltaban las abejas para dejar su miel
en los labios resecos y sin esperanzas
en los labios hundidos bajo las palabras
llenas de amor y sangre.

Nuestras cabezas acaban por perderse
envueltas en las nubes
la mía inclinada sobre el aire
la suya hecha amor por mis ojos.

When We Look at Each Other

My head leaned over the air
I looked at her head turned to love by my eyes
when from her hair
the bees flew to leave honey
on the dry lips and without hopes
in the sunken lips under the words
full of love and blood.

Our heads end up lost
covered in clouds
mine leaning over the air
hers turned to love by my eyes.

Las alas sirven para volar

Sólo un grano de anís puedo llevar sobre mi mano
porque mi mano es roja o blanca lo mismo que tu pecho
porque cuando la luz hunde los barcos
nos abandonamos en esta selva virgen que nos rodea
hasta oír el latido del árbol que tiene hojas de alas de pájaro
del árbol hecho con todos los corazones de los pájaros.

Después este grano de anís era la Muerte
recién salida de un cascarón blanco
hallado entre la arena de la playa
momentos antes del fusilamiento de Torrijos
mientras se hundía en tierra la sombra desgarrada
del único árbol que su savia es sangre de los pájaros.

Antes de que amanezca
vendrá a dejar su sangre una paloma blanca sobre nuestro tejado
y esa sangre cuajada a las doce del día podrá ser nuestra piel.

Wings are made for flying

Only an anis seed can I carry in my hand
because my hand is the same red or white as your breast
because when the light sinks the boats
they abandon us in a virgin forest that surrounds us
hearing the beat of the tree with leaves of bird wings
a tree made of bird hearts.

After the anis seed was Death
recently emerged from a white shell
found in beach sand
moments before the execution of Torrijos;
meanwhile the dissolute shadow of the lone tree
whose sap is bird's blood sinks in the earth.

Before dawn
a white dove will come to leave blood on our roof
and that blood, curdled, by noon will be our skin.

Granadas de fuego

Esta granada abierta que está entre nuestras manos
tiene dientes de sangre y carne de ballena
y ahora conserva intacta su agria arquitectura
porque fue desertora de las últimas guerras.

Entre vallados negros de gemidos y olas
sus granos desgranados iluminan la tierra
rompiendo oscuridades con su roja sonrisa
en el perfil agudo del agua sin conciencia.

Con sus ascuas de nieve calcina la alegría
sobre un piso de mármol de alguna ciudad eterna
para dejar desnudas verdades en pirámides
de tempestad y miedo ondear sus banderas.

Esta granada abierta no es el fruto de un árbol
que se engendró en el vientre de mares y de selvas;
en su cáscara amarga tiene amplitud de cielo
y en sus entrañas pican la aves y las fieras.

Pomegranates of Fire

This split pomegranate in our hands
has bloody teeth and whale's flesh
and now preserves a bitter architecture
because it was a deserter in the last wars.

Within black barricades of moans and waves
the pomegranate seeds illuminate the earth
breaking darkness with its red smile,
the sharp profile of heartless water.

With hot embers of snow it blackens happiness
on a marble floor of some eternal city
leaving naked truths in stormy pyramids
and fear waving its flags

This opened pomegranate isn't the fruit of a tree
bred in belly of seas and jungles;
in its bitter shell it carries the amplitude of the sky
and at its core peck birds and beasts.

De norte a sur

Mientras que los caballos corren por las praderas
y los barcos piratas se esconden entre hielos
guardando sus tesoros bajo las noches blancas
oigo una voz que canta muy cerca de mi pecho
una canción perdida a orilla de las aguas.

Un rumor imposible nacido de las hojas
verdes de los castaños escuchan mis oídos
y unas manos secaban el sudor de mi frente
con la bandera blanca de algún barco vencido
por los barcos piratas anclados en la nieve.

A través de los mares llevé las cabelleras
de las vírgenes negras muertas junto a la costa
con sus labios de fuego cubiertos por la sangre
de un capitán pirata sepultado en las olas
ardientes y saladas de mares tropicales.

Dormido en la cubierta bajo los cielos rasos
a la luz de luna que clavaba en mis huesos
una canción traída por lejanos amores
vi florecer las aguas de labios y de besos
y vi cómo una lluvia de pájaros y flores
nos caía en la frente y humedeció los sueños.

Mientras que los caballos corren por las praderas
y están presos los barcos entre mares helados
tienen su vista fija todos los marineros
sobre la Cruz de Sur que derramó en mis labios
una voz que cantaba muy cerca de mi pecho.

From north to south

While the horses run through the meadows
and the pirate ships hide in the ice
guarding their treasures under the white nights
I hear a voice sing from within my heart
a lost song to the water's shore.

My ears hear an impossible murmur
born in the green leaves of the chestnuts
and my hands dry the sweat from my face
with the white flag of some ship defeated
by the those of the pirates anchored in the snow.

Through the seas I carried the long hair
of the black virgins along the coast
their lips of fire covered by the blood
of a pirate captain buried in the burning and
salty waves of the tropical waters.

Asleep on the deck under clear skies
of moon light that fixed in my bones
a song of far-off lovers
I saw the waters of lips and kisses flower
and I saw how a rain of birds and flowers
fell before us and dampened our dreams.

While the horses run through the meadow
the ships are trapped in frozen seas,
all the sailors have their vision fixed
on the Southern Cross and from my lips spilled
a voice that sang from my heart.

El aire viene hasta nosotros

Rota la piel saltaba el fuego de mi carne
y rompía su llama la oscuridad eterna
que cubrirá los huesos de aquellos que en sus ojos
oculten entre ramas una palabra ciega.

Como el viento se hundía dentro de mis entrañas
y las nubes llevaban la savia de mi cuerpo
en todas las montañas florecían volcanes
y eran todas las piedras manantiales de fuego.

Rota la piel los aires aventaban mi carne
dolorida y alegre por el agua y la tierra
con el convencimiento de alcanzar algún día
la libertad prendida en cerco de banderas.

Al ir sólo la sangre sola por las montañas
pierde su color rojo entre piedras y árboles
y su voz se confunde con las voces de pájaros
llovidas de los cielos en mis cinco ciudades.

Pero esta llama inmensa calcinará los miembros
de las generaciones nacidas bajo el ritmo
eterno que desgranan las ametralladoras
sobre heridas abiertas en cuerpos doloridos.

Until the air arrives

From my broken skin jumped fire of my flesh
and its flame broke the eternal darkness
that will cover the bones of those in whose eyes
hide a blind word between branches.

As the wind buried itself deep within me
and the clouds carried my body's essence
volcanoes flowered in all the mountains
and they were rocky fountains of fire.

My skin broken the airs fanned my flesh
aching and happy by water and earth
with the certainty of a day in which
liberty would be seized from a ring of flags.

The blood alone goes to the mountains
loses its red color among the rocks and trees
and its voice is confused with the voices of birds
rained from the skies of my five cities.

But this immense flame will blacken the members
of our generation born under the eternal rhythm
that the machine guns thresh
on the open wounds of our aching bodies.

El fuego calcina nuestras carnes

Este brazo de fuego
quemaba mi costado
recubierto de brotes
plenos de savia verde
cuando tu cabellera
fue de piedra en el viento
y mis sueños se abrían
en pétalos de carne.

Estos aires de fuego
derretirán la nieve
lejana de los polos
al cuajar en el árbol
nuestros dos corazones.

The Fire Blackens Our Bodies

This arm of fire
burned my side
covered by buds
full of green sap
when your long hair
was stone in the wind
and my dreams opened
in petals of flesh.

Those airs of fire
will melt the poles'
distant snows,
when in the tree
our two hearts congeal.

Canción para cantar en primavera

Se albergan mis oídos
dentro de aquellas dos palomas blancas
escapadas, huidas de su cabeza rubia.

Traen la luz a mi deseo de siempre
murmullos de cristales y de plumas
y mi deseo de siempre
ve posarse las gotas de rocío
en sus ojos abiertos
en su cabeza rubia
y en tierra removida por sus sueños.
Las palomas se alejan
y se elevan entre nubes de hielo
apagando esta sed que seca mi garganta
con sus alas de agua
con las ramas de un árbol
brotadas a la sombra de mis manos.

Florecía el amor en su cabeza rubia
como la miel brotaba de las llagas de Cristo.

Song to sing in spring

My eyes take shelter
within those two white doves, escaped,
fled from your blonde head.

They carry the light of my constant desire,
murmur of crystal and feathers
and my constant desire
sees the dew drops settling
in your open eyes
on your blonde head
sees the earth stirred by your dreams.
The doves go on
rise between the clouds of ice
quenching this thirst that dries my throat
with its wings of water
with branches from a tree
sprung from the shadows of my hands.

Love flowered in your blonde head
like honey sprung from the wounds of Christ.

Árboles en mi vida

Desgarraba mi carne,
los dientes se clavaban en el hielo,
buscando entre sus fibras
hasta dónde llegaban las raíces
de este árbol negro
que sin piedad taladra mis sentidos.

La dirección del viento
la señalaba con el dedo índice
pero mi dedo índice
es la serpiente carne de mi carne
que hunde sus raíces
hasta perderse dentro de la tierra.

Mi corteza
o la de aquellos árboles que nos daban su sombra
lleva grabado un nombre
en todos los idiomas
del cual manará sangre eternamente.

Con los dientes clavados en el hielo
y los dedos crispados
¿conseguirán estas hachas de piedra
romper nuestras cadenas?

Trees in my life

My torn flesh
teeth nailed to the ice
looking among the fibers
for where the roots
of the black tree arrived
that without pity pierces my senses.

The wind's direction
known with the index finger
but that finger
is the serpent flesh of my flesh
that buries its roots
until losing itself in the earth.

The bark of my tree
or or one of those that shaded us
is engraved in all languages
with a name
from which blood will forever flow.

With teeth nailed to ice
and convulsed fingers
can they find those axes of stone
able to break our chains?

Abejas en su voz

En su voz se engendraban las abejas que pueblan mi cabeza
aire rubio que orea el esqueleto blanco de los sueños
aire lleno de gestos abandonados por su indiferencia
al nacer de las hostias esa luz que ilumina nuestro aliento.

Bees in your voice

From your voice came the bees that bred and lived inside my
    head
blonde air cools the white skeleton of dreams
air full of gestures, abandoned through indifference,
by the birth from out of of the hosts of that light that illuminates
    our breath.

Donde está nuestro destino

Estas inmensas almas que rodean mi vista
tienen en sus entrañas acero derretido
y sus granos de arena son las gotas de sangre
que vertió en nuestra frente el costado de Cristo.

Las voces se deshacen bajo el agua salada
filtrada por los besos perdidos en las noches
pobladas con brillantes ojos de enamorados
y llegan a mi oído en un rumor salobre.

¿Cuál es el horizonte que envuelve nuestra vida
cuando las caravanas huyen tras las fronteras
hundidas en la niebla sin dedos luminosos
para palpar el aire de nuestras calaveras?

Si nuestra sangre corre por los cauces resecos
de la tierra sedienta calcinada en las llamas
del amor diluido en desiertos de arena
¿cuál es nuestro destino en la roca tallada?

En la sombra de un árbol de raíces profundas
se reflejan las ramas rojas de nuestra sangre
y los labios abiertos de fatigas y espanto
beben agua de Cristo brotada de los mares.

Where our destiny lies

These immense souls that surround my view
have within them melted steel
and their grains of sand are drops of blood
that poured before us from the side of Christ.

The voices break up under the salt water
filtered by lost kisses in the nights
crowded with brilliance of the eyes of lovers
and with a briny murmur they reach my ears.

What is the horizon that encloses our lives
when the caravans flee for the frontiers
buried in the mists without luminous fingers
to feel the air of our skulls?

If our blood runs from dry river beds
of thinly blackened earth in the flames
of love diluted in deserts of sand
what is our destiny in the carved rock?

In the shadow of a deep rooted tree
the red branches reflect our blood
and the open lips of fatigue and terror
drink the water of Christ springing from the seas.

Katherine Koch is a painter whose work has been shown internationally and is privately collected. In addition to her current work as a painter, she is writing a memoir of growing up in Greenwich Village, NY as one of the children of the New York School of Poets.

Willis Barnstone is the author of seventy books; recent volumes are *Poetics of Translation* (Yale, 1995), *The Gnostic Bible* (Shambhala, 2003), *Life Watch* (BOA, 2003), *Border of a Dream: Selected Poems of Antonio Machado* (2004), *Restored New Testament* (Norton, 2009), *Stickball on 88th Street* (Red Hen Press, 2011), *Dawn Café in Paris* (Sheep Meadow, 2011), and *The Poems of Jesus Christ* (Norton, 2012). Born in Lewiston, Maine, Barnstone was educated at Bowdoin, the Sorbonne, Columbia and Yale. He taught in Greece at end of civil war (1949-51), in Buenos Aires during the Dirty War, and in China during Cultural Revolution, where he was later a Fulbright Professor in Beijing (1984-85). Former O'Connor Professor of Greek at Colgate University, he is Distinguished Professor of Comparative Literature at Indiana University. A Guggenheim fellow, he has received the NEA, NEH, Emily Dickinson Award of the PSA, Auden Award of NY Council on the Arts, Midland Authors Award, four Book of the Month selections, and four Pulitzer nominations. His work has appeared in *APR*, *Harper's*, *NYRB*, *Paris Review*, *Poetry*, *New Yorker*, *TLS*.

Available from
UNOPRESS

General Titles

The Not Yet by Moira Crone, 978-1-60801-072-1 (2012)

A Baltic Anthology Book 1: Contemporary Latvian Poetry, edited by Inara Cedrins, 978-1-60801-050-9 (2012)

A Baltic Anthology Book 2: Contemporary Estonian Poetry, edited by Inara Cedrins, 978-1-60801-052-3 (2012)

A Baltic Anthology Book 3: Contemporary Lithuanian Poetry, edited by Inara Cedrins, 978-1-60801-051-6 (2012)

The Astral Plane: Stories of Cuba, the Southwest and Beyond by Teresa Dovalpage, 978-1-60801-078-3 (2012)

The Man Who Wanted to Buy a Heart by Leonard S. Bernstein, 978-1-60801-073-8 (2012)

Post-Katrina Brazucas: Brazilian Immigrants in New Orleans by Annie McNeill Gibson, 978-1-60801-070-7 (2011)

New Orleans: The Underground Guide (2nd Edition) by Michael Patrick Welch & Alison Fensterstock, 978-1-60801-079-0 (2011)

The Saratoga Collection, edited by Terrence Sanders, 978-1-60801-061-5 (2011)

The Garden Path: The Miseducation of a City, by Andre Perry, 978-1-60801-048-6 (2011)

Before (During) After: Louisiana Photographers Visual Reactions to Hurricane Katrina, edited by Elizabeth Kleinveld, 978-1-60801-023-3 (2010)

Beyond the Islands by Alicia Yánez Cossío, translated by Amalia Gladhart, 978-1-60801-043-1 (2010)

The Fox's Window by Naoko Awa, translated by Toshiya Kamei,978-1-60801-006-6 (2010)

Black Santa by Jamie Bernstein, 978-1-60801-022-6 (2010)

Dream-crowned (Traumgekrönt) by Rainer Maria Rilke, translated by Lorne Mook, 978-1-60801-041-7 (2010)

Voices Rising II: More Stories from the Katrina Narrative Project edited by Rebeca Antoine, 978-0-9706190-8-2 (2010)

Rowing to Sweden: Essays on Faith, Love, Politics, and Movies by Fredrick Barton, 978-1-60801-001-1 (2010)

Dogs in My Life: The New Orleans Photographs by John Tibule Mendes, 978-1-60801-005-9 (2010)

New Orleans: The Underground Guide by Michael Patrick Welch & Alison Fensterstock, 978-1-60801-019-6 (2010)

Understanding the Music Business: A Comprehensive View edited by Harmon Greenblatt & Irwin Steinberg, 978-1-60801-004-2 (2010)

The Gravedigger by Rob Magnuson Smith, 978-1-60801-010-3 (2010)

Portraits: Photographs in New Orleans 1998-2009 by Jonathan Traviesa, 978-0-9706190-5-1 (2009)

I hope it's not over, and good-by: Selected Poems of Everette Maddox by Everette Maddox, 978-1-60801-000-4 (2009)

Theoretical Killings: Essays & Accidents by Steven Church, 978-0-9706190-6-8 (2009)

Voices Rising: Stories from the Katrina Narrative Project edited by Rebeca Antoine, 978-0-9728143-6-2 (2008)

On Higher Ground: The University of New Orleans at Fifty by Dr. Robert Dupont, 978-0-9728143-5-5 (2008)

The Change Cycle Handbook by Will Lannes, 978-0-9728143-9-3 (2008)

Us Four Plus Four: Eight Russian Poets Conversing translated by Don Mager, 978-0-9706190-4-4 (2008)

The El Cholo Feeling Passes by Fredrick Barton, 978-0-9728143-2-4 (2003)

A House Divided by Fredrick Barton, 978-0-9728143-1-7 (2003)

William Christenberry: Art & Family by J. Richard Gruber, 978-0-9706190-0-6 (2000)

The Neighborhood Story Project

New Orleans in 19 Movements by Thurgood Marshall Early College High School, 978-1-60801-069-1 (2011)

The Combination by Ashley Nelson, 978-1-60801-055-4 (2010)

Between Piety and Desire by Arlet Wylie and Sam Wylie, 978-1-60801-040-0 (2010)

The House of Dance and Feathers: A Museum by Ronald W. Lewis by Rachel Breunlin & Ronald W. Lewis, 978-0-9706190-7-5 (2009)

Beyond the Bricks by Daron Crawford & Pernell Russell, 978-1-60801-016-5 (2010)

Aunt Alice Vs. Bob Marley by Kareem Kennedy, 978-1-60801-013-4 (2010)

Signed, The President by Kenneth Phillips, 978-1-60801-015-8 (2010)

Houses of Beauty: From Englishtown to the Seventh Ward by Susan Henry, 978-1-60801-014-1 (2010)

Coming Out the Door for the Ninth Ward edited by Rachel Breunlin, 978-0-9706190-9-9 (2006)

Cornerstones: Celebrating the Everyday Monuments & Gathering Places of New Orleans edited by Rachel Breunlin, 978-0-9706190-3-7 (2008)

The Engaged Writers Series

Medea and Her War Machines by Ioan Flora, translated by Adam J. Sorkin, 978-1-60801-067-7 (2011)

Together by Julius Chingono and John Eppel, 978-1-60801-049-3

Available from
PRESS

(2011)

Vegetal Sex (O Sexo Vegetal) by Sergio Medeiros, translated by Raymond L.Bianchi, 978-1-60801-046-2 (2010)

Wounded Days (Los Días Heridos) by Leticia Luna, translated by Toshiya Kamei, 978-1-60801-042-4 (2010)

When the Water Came: Evacuees of Hurricane Katrina by Cynthia Hogue & Rebecca Ross, 978-1-60801-012-7 (2010)

A Passenger from the West by Nabile Farès, translated by Peter Thompson, 978-1-60801-008-0 (2010)

Everybody Knows What Time It Is by Reginald Martin, 978-1-60801-011-0 (2010)

Green Fields: Crime, Punishment, & a Boyhood Between by Bob Cowser, Jr., 978-1-60801-018-9 (2010)

Open Correspondence: An Epistolary Dialogue by Abdelkébir Khatibi and Rita El Khayat, translated by Safoi Babana-Hampton, Valérie K. Orlando, Mary Vogl, 978-1-60801-021-9 (2010)

Gravestones (Lápidas) by Antonio Gamoneda, translated by Donald Wellman, 978-1-60801-002-8 (2009)

Hearing Your Story: Songs of History and Life for Sand Roses by Nabile Farès translated by Peter Thompson, 978-0-9728143-7-9 (2008)

The Katrina Papers: A Journal of Trauma and Recovery by Jerry W. Ward, Jr., 978-0-9728143-3-1 (2008)

Contemporary Poetry

Sheer Indefinite: Selected Poems 1991-2011 by Skip Fox, 978-1-60801-080-6 (2011)

Atlanta Poets Group Anthology: The Lattice Inside by Atlanta Poets Group, 978-1-60801-064-6 (2011)

Makebelieve by Caitlin Scholl, 978-1-60801-056-1 (2011)

California Redemption Value by Kevin Opstedal, 978-1-60801-066-0 (2011)

Dear Oxygen: New and Selected Poems by Lewis MacAdams, edited by Kevin Opstedal, 978-1-60801-059-2 (2011)

Only More So by Tony Lopez, 978-1-60801-057-8 (2011)

Enridged by Brian Richards, 978-1-60801-047-9 (2011)

The Ezra Pound Center for Literature

Modernism and the Orient, edited by Zhaoming Qian, 978-1-60801-074-5 (2012)

A Gallery of Ghosts by John Gery, 978-0-9728143-4-8 (2008)

The Poets of the Sala Capizucchi (I Poeti della Sala Capizucchi), edited by Caterina Ricciardi and John Gery, 978-1-60801-068-4 (2011)

Trespassing, by Patrizia de Rachewiltz, 978-1-60801-060-8 (2011)

The Imagist Poem: Modern Poetry in Miniature edited by William Pratt, 978-0-9728143-8-6 (2008)